Career advancement and change
go hand in hand.
You can't have one
without the other.

By accepting a promotion,
you took on a new role ...
a new set of responsibilities.

And you must deal with the fact that —
in the eyes of employees —
you are no longer "one of us."

WALK
THE TALK

Trusted Books. Positive Results.

PEER TODAY, BOSS TOMORROW

Inquiries regarding permission for use of the material contained in this book should be sent to info@walkthetalk.com.

WALK THE TALK books may be purchased for educational, business, or sales promotion use.

Printed in the United States of America
20 19 18 17 16

Produced by Steve Ventura
Edited by Michelle Sedas

ISBN 1-885228-69-4

ACKNOWLEDGMENTS

Special thanks to
ERIC HARVEY and **STEVE VENTURA**
for providing the input, support,
and encouragement that
helped make this book a reality...

...and to the wonderful leaders,
mentors, and coworkers who – over the
years – made it possible for me to
transition from peer to boss.

INTRODUCTION

Chances are the words still echo in your memory:

"Congratulations ... welcome to management!"

Those words (or others like them) are validation that your past efforts as an "individual contributor" have paid off. You worked hard, did a good job, kept your nose clean, and YOU GOT PROMOTED! And as a result – no matter if your title is *Manager, Supervisor, Team Lead* (or something similar) – you're in charge ... you are "the boss."

The *good news* about your promotion: **things changed.** Now YOU are calling more of the shots, setting the tone, and directing the work of others. You undoubtedly are more privy to information about the business, and you're probably enjoying more latitude and a few more perks than ever before.

The *bad news* about your promotion: **things changed!** You took on a whole new set of duties and responsibilities (often accompanied by longer hours) that require special skills – ones that are different from the *technical* know-how you developed in previous jobs ... and that probably helped get you promoted in the first place. But perhaps the biggest change of all is one of workplace *relationships*. The coworkers who used to be your "peers" are now the employees who report to you. And the fact is that even if they were happy that "one of us got promoted" when you got the job, you're no longer in that "us." Now, you have a different group of peers ... now you *are* **management!**

Making the transition from employee to supervisor can be one of the hardest things any of us ever has to do in our careers. At times, the additional responsibilities (and accountabilities) of being "the boss" can leave you feeling overwhelmed, alone, maybe even a little panicky, and wondering if you did the right thing by accepting the promotion – regardless of how recent, or long ago, that might have been. If that's the case, take a deep breath and relax. Help has arrived!

Within the pages that follow, you'll find four specific strategies to help you successfully navigate your changing role and meet the challenges that come with your supervisory position. You'll learn how to:

1 **ACCEPT YOUR LEADERSHIP ROLE** and all that comes with it.

2 **SET CLEAR BOUNDARIES** for all to follow.

3 **COMMUNICATE** more effectively with everyone you lead.

4 **TAKE ACTION** to get the results you want and need.

Whether you're a seasoned supervisor, you're newly promoted (and wondering *What do I do now?*), or you're preparing yourself for a future leadership position, this book is for you. By *applying* the information you're about to read, you'll reduce any fears or frustration you may be feeling, increase your personal effectiveness and professional reputation, gain greater respect from the people reporting to you, and enhance your overall career.

Most importantly, you'll prove to everyone (including yourself) that you ARE the kind of leader that others will want to follow.

CONTENTS

Strategy 1

ACCEPT YOUR LEADERSHIP ROLE

**The first step toward change is awareness.
The second step is acceptance.**

~ Nathaniel Branden

As a supervisor, it's imperative that you accept the fact that your duties and accountabilities, your workplace relationships, and the way your value to the organization is measured all changed the moment you were promoted

Now, you are "the leader." And that reality must be reflected in your attitude, your approach, and — most importantly — through your behaviors.

The New Supervision

In the past, organizations placed primary importance on technical expertise when it came to promotions. Supervisors were expected to be well-skilled in every aspect of the work done by the people they managed – that's how they got to be "the boss." Typically, the best nurse became the nursing supervisor; the super salesperson was named sales manager; the top-notch welder moved up to shift lead, and so forth. For these folks, it was presumed that knowing employees' jobs better than the employees them-selves was the key to management success. In *today's* complex and com-petitive business arena, however, the requirements have changed and intensified. As a result, supervisors must provide more than just technical knowledge. They must also be skilled in arenas such as administration, performance management, and leadership. The "trade" has changed – and so have "the tools of the trade."

A Different Value

Before you were promoted, your value to the organization was measured by what you, as an *individual*, could do successfully. Your contribution came through the quality and quantity of the work you were hired to do – whether that entailed providing services or creating products. YOU, along with your fellow employees, produced the results by which you were evaluated. As a supervisor, however, your value to the organization is assessed differently. It's no longer about how successful *you* are in what you do. Now it's about how successful your direct reports are – **because** of what you do. Now, you have a different purpose ... a revised focus ... a new overall goal:

getting results *through* others.

Different Duties

Think about the title "supervisor" for a moment. What is it that supervisors do? The simple answer is *supervise*. And that begs the natural, follow-up question: What/who do supervisors supervise? The answer to that one should be obvious: *people!* So it's no surprise that, once promoted, a sizable portion of your time will (or at least *should*) focus on "people management" activities.

Accepting your leadership role means understanding that your "to-do list" looks much different than it did as a non-management employee. Now, that list includes things like hiring, coaching, counseling, communicating, directing, developing, evaluating, disciplining, and perhaps even the dreaded "f word": firing. You need to be adept at these activities, knowledgeable about the policies and procedures that guide them, and willing to do whatever is appropriate whenever it's called for. And that's just the *people* side of your job! You also must manage and oversee the *work* that is done by those people as well. So, also included in your to-do's are activities such as planning, scheduling, implementing, and monitoring – tasks you'll also need to be well-versed in.

How do you acquire/enhance the knowledge and skills you need for these different duties and responsibilities? Here are a few ideas:

Ask your manager to help you develop by sharing supervisory tips and techniques he or she has learned over time.

Talk with other supervisors to learn what they do, what they know, and what they've experienced.

Overall, **take responsibility** for your own leadership development and make it a top priority.

Changed Relationships and Allegiances

By accepting a promotion, you gave up membership in one "club" and took on membership in another. Your old club was comprised of non-management employees ... individual contributors. These were your coworkers, fellow team members and, in many cases, your friends. Chances are you joked together, took breaks together, looked out for each other, and occasionally complained about management to each other. You were a member in good standing of that peer worker group known as "us." But all that changed the moment you became a supervisor. You're no longer one of the guys (or girls). Now you're one of the "them" you used to commiserate about ... now, you're management. And your primary allegiance must be to the organization and its overall mission.

A COMMON CONCERN

Question: **Does being a supervisor mean that I must abandon coworker friendships I developed and enjoyed as an employee?**

Answer: **Not at all!** It does mean, however, that you and your friends must accept the fact that your relationships are different *at work* ... that you're the boss. As long as you offer no special treatment, your friends expect none, and you avoid any improprieties, old friendships can (and should) continue.

Just remember that this can become a "slippery slope." Should you ever find yourself having to choose between doing your job or keeping a friend, your allegiance must be to the job. But then, a *true* friend would never put you in that position to begin with.

Joining the ranks of management not only results in changes to *old* workplace relationships, it also produces many *new* ones as well. Along with your supervisory position came a new group of counterparts ... a different set of peers ... a new "us" that you'll need to learn about, work with, and rely on for assistance. And, because your leadership role is more pervasive and "big picture" oriented than it was as an employee (individual contributor), there are many people in other departments and d visions – and some from outside of your organization – with whom you must communicate, coordinate, and cooperate. The diagram below provides a sampling of groups and individuals you may work with on any given day:

Being familiar with the additional contacts and new relationships that came with your promotion is critical to your success as a supervisor. So, confer with your manager and other supervisors. Develop a list of all the people you may need to interface with. If you haven't already done so, contact each person on the list to introduce yourself. And schedule a time when you can meet, get to know each other, learn about his or her operation, and discuss what you need to do in order to work productively ... together.

Additional Accountabilities

Go back and take a look at the job description or job posting sheet for your supervisory position. Chances are that: 1) you'll see a list of duties, tasks, and expectations that are much different than what was required of you as an individual contributor, and 2) you're responsible – and *accountable* – for all of the items listed on that document ... and more.

What does it mean to be accountable? It means that you must oversee, direct, control, and "answer for" what happens within a specified area of activity. Obviously, you're accountable for your own performance and conduct. And, as a supervisor, you're also accountable for the behavior and performance of your direct reports – and the results they achieve (or fail to achieve). But your responsibilities don't end there. More "come with the territory" – such as handling budget issues, managing overtime, maintaining the confidentiality of sensitive information, and protecting the facility, equipment, and organizational resources. There are safety issues, legal issues, compliance issues, ethical issues – all of which you're expected to know about and handle properly.

Certainly, supervisors' responsibilities will vary from organization to organization and from position to position – as will the guidelines that apply to them. Here are a few things you can do to get a handle on what YOU are accountable for:

✓ Ask your manager and other supervisors;

✓ Confer with representatives from other departments such as Legal, Finance, Human Resources, and those you work with on a regular basis;

✓ Request copies of – and become thoroughly familiar with – all organizational **policies, procedures, and regulations** that apply to your job as a leader.

Demonstrating Your Acceptance

To be an effective supervisor, you not only need to accept your leadership role, you also need to *demonstrate* that you've accepted it. How do you do that? Through specific behaviors like the following:

Become a "learning machine." Ask your manager to help you create a personal development plan for building/enhancing the knowledge, skills, and relationships necessary for success as a supervisor. Study all applicable policy and procedure manuals supplied by your organization. Make sure you fully understand the duties, responsibilities, and senior-management expectations that came with your job. Take advantage of any mentoring programs and leadership-development resources (books, videos, training classes, etc.) available through your organization. And make a special effort to learn "the business of the business." The more you know about the various functions and activities that make your organization tick, the better you'll be able to contribute as an important member of management.

Do your job – not your employees'. Your management duties can truly be challenging. There may be times when you're unsure of what you're doing ... when your confidence is shaken. And because you want to make a contribution and feel good about yourself, there's a temptation to call upon your old technical skills, jump in, and start doing the work your employees are now supposed to do. Avoid that trap! Sure, you should pitch in if people get in a real bind. But don't make a habit of it. Remember that you're a supervisor. Whenever you're doing employee work, no one is doing yours.

Lead by example. Model the behaviors you expect from your direct reports. If you expect others to be on time, work hard, follow the rules, and "go the extra mile" – you must do those things yourself. Your employees will be watching you. And they'll rightfully assume that it's okay for them to do whatever you do.

Avoid finger pointing. Never question or criticize your organization's policies, or its leadership, in front of your direct reports – regardless of how disturbed you may be. If you have a concern, take it up with the people who can do something about it. And, by all means, refuse to get involved in workplace "pity parties" that do nothing but celebrate problems and encourage dissention. As a supervisor, your allegiance must be with management – not your old buddies.

Along that same line ...

Don't pass the buck. Avoid "Teflon-coated" phrases like *It wasn't my idea; I didn't make the rule;* or *Don't blame me* – intended to keep you in good favor with your employees (at others' expense). They don't work. Worse yet, they erode your authority as a leader.

When in doubt, ASK! Supervising others is an important job. The actions you take, and decisions you make, impact the organization in general – and your employees (and customers) in particular. So don't wing it, fake it, or guess. If you're not sure what to do in any given situation, confer with someone who knows.

Strategy

2

SET CLEAR BOUNDARIES

**Without a road map and a clear understanding
of the "rules of the road," it can be much harder
for employees to get to where they need to go.**

~ Eric Harvey

Along with your promotion came many changes to accept and deal
with — not only for you, but for each of your direct reports as well.
And it's up to you to orchestrate the adjustment process by establishing your authority, clarifying expectations, and helping everyone
on the team — especially former peers — understand how your relationships have been redefined.

"Sizing up" The Boss

If there's one thing most employees know for sure, it's that no two supervisors are exactly the same. While roles and responsibilities may be similar, each leader comes to the job with his or her own style and personality – and collection of expectations, insecurities, pet peeves, hot buttons, and taboos. So it should be no surprise that team members will want (and need) to size you up by answering questions such as:

How strong a leader is he or she?
What's important to him or her?
What does he or she want from me?
How do I stay on his or her good side ... and out of trouble?
Where does he or she "draw the line"?

It can be challenging for everyone – including you – as this time of discovery plays itself out. Some of *your* challenges may come from former peers who are testing the waters to see how and where things stand between you – and whether or not your past relationship will affect the way you supervise them.

Obviously, your management position necessitates adjustments on the part of employees as well as yours. They must see, through your actions and behaviors, that you are in charge ... that you take your leadership position seriously. So, you'll need to set the tone and redefine your relationship by **setting clear boundaries** – as quickly as possible – that help employees understand the "ground rules" that apply to EVERYONE.

Boundaries: The Whats and Whys

A somewhat common misconception floating around the land of leadership is that establishing boundaries is an in-your-face activity that involves telling employees *Don't do this* and *You better not do that*. As a result of the perceived negative connotations, many supervisors – especially *new* supervisors – are uncomfortable with the task. Some avoid it altogether – unfairly requiring their team members to figure things out on their own. But it doesn't need to be that way ... it *shouldn't* be that way!

Fact is, setting boundaries is less about identifying what NOT to do and more about clarifying expectations. The process involves meeting with your direct reports and clearly communicating:

What you expect of them
How they should do their jobs and conduct themselves

and ...

What they can expect from you
How you will respond to their behavior and performance.

The act of setting boundaries (clarifying expectations) is beneficial in many ways. *First,* it establishes your authority as a leader who is committed to managing effectively. *Second,* it reinforces the need for employees to perform well and contribute to the organization. *Third,* it helps former peers understand the nature of your "new" relationship. *Fourth,* and most importantly, it gives everyone on the team a road map to success.

The "Big Two"

When establishing boundaries, there are two primary areas that you should focus on:

POLICIES and PROCEDURES

These are the organizational rules and regulations – typically in written form – designed to ensure a safe, efficient, consistent, and regulatory-compliant business operation. Examples include:

- Safety and material-handling regulations.
- Documentation and reporting procedures.
- Confidentiality requirements for sensitive information.
- Work processes and quality standards.
- Laws and Codes of Ethics.

BEHAVIORS and ACTIONS

These are the "conduct" guidelines – sometimes written, sometimes not – that reflect behaviors the organization sees as appropriate and correct on the job. Examples include:

- Punctuality and attendance.
- Adherence to dress codes.
- Respectful treatment of coworkers, customers, and suppliers.
- Honesty in all business activities.
- Maintaining service standards.
- Collaboration with other departments.

SETTING BOUNDARIES CHECKLIST

❑ Make sure that your direct reports have copies of all written policies, procedures, regulations, and behavioral guidelines that apply to them and their jobs.

❑ Create and distribute a list of any informal ("unwritten") rules and requirements that also apply.

Then, meet with your direct reports and do the following:

❑ Review and discuss the guidelines. Ask questions to confirm employee understanding.

❑ Clarify your expectation that everyone on the team will strictly adhere to all policies, procedures, and behavioral guidelines – without exception.

❑ Explain the importance of these requirements and the impact on the organization when they are ignored/violated. Affirm your commitment to them.

❑ Clarify that it's your obligation to enforce the rules – and explain what everyone can expect from you when the rules are followed … and when they aren't.

The Importance of Consistency

Here's a truism to remember: rules and guidelines are meaningful only when they are followed ... when they are enforced. So, when it comes to setting boundaries, *stating* your expectations of employees is only half the battle. The other half involves "delivering" on what you tell employees to expect from you. You must *walk* the talk. And the key to doing that is **consistency** – holding ALL the people accountable for following ALL the rules (boundaries), ALL the time.

It's critically important that you address each policy, procedure, or behavioral guideline violation as soon as you become aware of it. The type of meeting you have with the employee – and the resulting consequences – may vary based on the history and severity of the problem. What must not vary, however, is your practice of confronting issues. Let some things (or people) slide, and you run many risks, including:

- Sending mixed and confusing messages to the people who depend upon you for guidance and direction.

- Creating a workplace where employees decide which rules are important and which ones can be "stretched" or ignored.

- Exposing yourself to charges of favoritism or discrimination.

- Losing the respect of the members of your team.

- Facing negative consequences from *your* boss for not doing your job.

The truth is, in order for employees to see and accept you as the leader, you must BE the leader. And that means not only talking about boundaries, but consistently enforcing them as well.

Setting Boundaries: Dos and Don'ts

DO ...

- Make sure that you are totally familiar with all of the policies, procedures, and rules *before* discussing them with your direct reports.

- Interpret organizational policies for employees. Help them understand how the regulations and guidelines apply to the work that they do.

- Communicate the *whys* as well as the *whats*. Let people know why the rules exist, what benefits they provide to everyone, and how the organization is negatively impacted when they are not followed.

- Meet individually with former peers who now report to you. Clarify your intention to enforce the rules fairly and consistently. Tell them you need their support in your leadership role. Ask them to serve as role models for others on the team to follow when it comes to respecting the boundaries.

- Stand your ground and hold everyone accountable.

And by all means ...

- Recognize, reinforce, and thank direct reports who respect the boundaries. Make sure you "do right by those who do right." There should be positive consequences for *following* the rules just as there are negative consequences for *violating* them.

DON'T ...

- Let your personal feelings sidetrack you from establishing boundaries and enforcing the rules.

- Let "buddies" come before business. Remember that if forced to take sides, your allegiance must be to the organization – no matter how difficult that may be.

- Evaluate or assign levels of importance to policies, procedures, and guidelines. By adopting the mindset that all rules are *equally* important, you'll avoid the trap of allowing "minor" violations to become acceptable.

- Assume that "once is enough" when it comes to discussing policies, procedures, and guidelines with your direct reports. Instead, make it a recurring topic of conversation at staff meetings and coaching sessions.

- Share privileged or confidential information with direct reports who are not in a need-to-know category. That includes "the one person I can tell anything to" (who also has one person he or she can tell anything to ... and so on). Remember that supervisors have boundaries, too.

- Initiate a formal response (discipline/discharge) to any rule or regulation violation without first conferring with the appropriate organizational resources and authorities.

Strategy 3

COMMUNICATE

The art of communication is the language of leadership.

~ James Humes

Think that communicating is mostly an occupational specialty for "English majors" who work in Public Relations, Marketing, and Communications departments? Think that good communicators are born, not made? If so, think again!

Fact is, communication is at the very core of people management. And the skills necessary to do it well can be developed by anyone. All it takes is knowledge, focus, commitment ... and practice!

It *IS* Your Job

Do you know which activity supervisors engage in the most? It's communicating! Combine all the time spent making and returning phone calls, sending and responding to e-mails, writing notes, memos, and reports, meeting with people (e.g., employees, managers, reps from other departments, customers, suppliers), making presentations, and the like, and you'll probably find that 70-90% of your total working hours involve some form of communication.

Truth is, you don't just engage in communication – you *rely* on it. It's the vehicle you use to ...

- **inform** people of things they need to know to do their jobs;

- **instruct** employees on the "whats" and "how wells" of the work to be done;

- **learn** what employees, customers, and other departments need;

- **clarify** expectations, roles, responsibilities, and time frames;

- **coach** direct reports to help them learn, improve, and grow;

- **motivate** your team to higher levels of performance and satisfaction;

- **receive and understand** input, feedback, questions, and concerns;

- **correct** performance and behavioral problems;

- **commend** and reinforce employees for doing well.

Communicating is your primary tool for leading people and achieving results. And since the majority of what you do involves communication, the majority of your success – and that of your people – will be built around how well you understand it ... and DO it.

Communication is actually a two-part process ... a two-way street. There are the messages you send to others – commonly referred to as "communication out," and the messages others send (or *try* to send) to you – which we call "communication in." While the first part tends to get the most attention and focus, both parts are equally important to your leadership effectiveness.

Communication OUT

Regardless of the content or format, the primary goal of communication is **understanding**. As a supervisor, you regularly will have thoughts, information, and/or concerns that you need to share with your direct reports – and others within the organization. Obviously, it's important that people hear and understand what you're saying. The messages they receive must be the same as the ones that you send. And to help make sure that happens, you need to:

Pay attention to WHAT YOU SAY.
Choose your words carefully. Use clear, direct language that people will understand. Avoid generalities ("a lot," "occasionally," etc.) that can be interpreted in different ways.

Pay attention to HOW YOU SAY IT.
Make sure your tone and body language are in sync with, and support, the words that you use.

> *Research on interpersonal communication indicates that, on average ...*
> 7% of all messages are communicated verbally – 93% are sent non-verbally.
> *And of the 93% non-verbal communication ...*
> 38% is through vocal tones – 55% is through facial expressions.

Pay attention to WHAT THEY HEAR
Confirm understanding. Ask questions to make sure that your message was received as you intended.

When it comes to communication, one style does *not* fit all. So, to help ensure that your messages are correctly understood, you need to vary your approach – depending on the preferences of the people you're communicating with. How do you determine which style people prefer? By observing how they, themselves, communicate over time.

Communication style preferences are based on two factors.

Directness – Some people prefer a straightforward approach and quick pace (more direct), while others respond better to less assertive words and a relaxed, conversational tempo (less direct).

Emotions/Sensitivity – For some individuals, sensitivity is not an issue – emotions and feelings are minor considerations in communication (less emotional). Other people, however, are higher on the sensitivity scale – with a much greater need to have their feelings considered (more emotional).

The chart below provides tips for communicating with different preferences.

LESS EMOTIONAL

Provide specifics • • Focus on results
Be organized • • Provide options
Stay on target • • Be concise
Allow for discussion of details • • Get to the point
Don't hurry the conversation • • Keep to the agenda

LESS DIRECT **MORE DIRECT**

Spend time informally • • Ask for their opinions and input
Allow for questions and feedback • • Piggyback/build on their ideas
Don't push or rush • • Compliment them
Show personal interest • • Share your excitement
Focus on people and teamwork • • Be open to socializing

MORE EMOTIONAL

Communication IN

Just as *you* have a need to be heard, so do your team members and others within the organization. Your colleagues and direct reports will be sharing many things with you – from ideas, suggestions, and explanations ... to problems, concerns, and questions. And it's critically important that you understand the messages that are sent your way. In order to *lead* effectively, you must be able to **listen** effectively.

Effective listening is an active process that requires attention and focus. It's important that you concentrate on the words and behaviors of the speaker – without passing immediate judgment. There will be plenty of time for evaluation of the message down the road.

The key, here, is remembering that the goal of communication is UNDER-STANDING – "I want to hear what you have to say" ... "I want to know what you are thinking and feeling" ... "I want to understand what the issues look like through your eyes." You don't have to agree with people's positions in order to understand where they're coming from and why they feel as they do. And once you have that knowledge, you'll be better able to work constructively with them and establish mutually beneficial relationships of success.

> Listening, not imitation, may be
> the sincerest form of flattery.
>
> ~ Dr. Joyce Brothers

So, what does effective listening entail? Actually, there are four key ingredients:

1. **Respect for the speaker.** Assume that what the person has to say is truly important to him or her. Put aside any negative attitudes or feelings you may have toward the individual. Approach the interaction with an open mind. Do your absolute best to remain objective and impartial.

2. **Attention to the speaker.** Stop whatever else you're doing and focus on what the person is saying. Eliminate distractions (turn off phones, pagers, etc.). Don't allow others to interrupt your conversation. If conditions aren't good for listening, change locations or schedule a different time to talk.

. **Appropriate body language.** Face the speaker and maintain eye contact. Lean forward. Nod as the person speaks. Avoid distracting behaviors such as finger tapping, doodling, sighing, or rolling your eyes.

. **Interaction with the speaker.** Repeat what you hear to verify your under-standing. Ask questions for clarification – and for obtaining additional infor-mation. *Demonstrate* that you're listening by saying things like: "I see," "uh-huh," "hmmm," and "I didn't know that."

PARAPHRASING

Unquestionably, the best technique for effective listening is paraphrasing: repeating, in your own words, what someone says – to that person's satisfaction. Example: *Deborah, let me make sure I understand. You're saying that .... Is that correct?*

Paraphrasing provides two distinct benefits. First, it helps ensure understanding. It just may be that what you heard is not what the person meant. Paraphrasing allows him or her to respond with either *Yes, that's what I'm saying,* or *No, that's not right. What I'm saying is ....* If it's the latter, you have an immediate opportunity for clarification. Second, paraphrasing is another way to **show** the person that you are listening and are making a sincere effort to get the message. That's reassuring; it helps eliminate tension and provides an incentive for the person to continue sharing his or her thoughts and feelings.

Additional Communication Tips and Techniques

For Communication OUT ...

Keep it real. Most people are turned-off by what they perceive as unrealistic claims, goals, and promises. There are no "cure alls" in the world ... and your coworkers know it. When it comes to communicating your messages, be positive and upbeat – tell it like you see it ... just don't "oversell" it.

Avoid "data dumps." Narrow your verbal and written communication down to no more than three key points. Bombard people with more information than they can handle (or remember) and they'll tune out.

Use a "what's in it for you" approach. Nothing fosters support and acceptance better than personal benefit. Emphasize how the subject of your communication (a plan, policy, decision, etc.) will benefit the audience and you'll increase receptivity for your message.

Find out how you're doing. Have team members and colleagues critique your communication skills. Ask everyone to respond (anonymously), in writing, to the following question: "What two things can I do to be a more effective communicator?" Thank people for their willingness to provide you with input. And make sure you ACT on the information you receive.

For Communication IN ...

Focus on content, not delivery. Remember that some people are more articulate than others. Certain employees may have difficulty expressing themselves – they may be awkward with phrases, they may misuse words, or they may take a long time to communicate simple ideas. Don't get hung up on their presentation. Assume they're doing the best they can, and look for every opportunity to be supportive and demonstrate patience. Just make sure that you don't speak for them.

Never interrupt. Interrupting – including finishing a person's sentences – is disrespectful, frustrating, and counterproductive to effective communication.

Watch for the "non-verbals." Pay attention to the speaker's body language. Does he or she seem nervous? Angry? Scared? Reflect on his or her feelings: *Johnny, I'm sensing that this is really disturbing for you. Can you tell me what you're feeling right now?* Addressing non-verbal communication can help draw out issues that might otherwise be left unspoken and unaddressed.

Think about *the speaker's* words. Avoid the common trap of planning *your* response while the person is speaking. If you catch yourself thinking about what you'll say as soon as he or she stops talking, immediately refocus on listening.

Strategy

4

TAKE ACTION

**Begin somewhere. You cannot build a
reputation on what you intend to do.**

~ Elizabeth Smith

Reflect, for a moment, on what it means to be a "boss." What's your
overall purpose? Why does your position exist?

If you're like most folks, there's a good chance you responded to
those questions with phrases such as: to supervise ... to manage ...
to lead. Those answers all have something in common: they involve
verbs — ACTION words. And that's no coincidence.

The Results/Action Imperative

Take any group of employees, without supervision, and they will perform at a certain level and accomplish certain things. Now, add a supervisor to the equation. What's your expectation? Obviously, the team members should perform at higher levels. If they don't, the boss isn't needed – he or she is drawing a salary but adding no value ... he or she is "dead weight." That's why the ultimate criteria for measuring management effectiveness is **results**!

Clearly, your job is to help direct reports be more successful in achieving the results your organization wants and needs. But that won't happen through osmosis. Nor will strong wishes and good intentions make it so. You must *do* things in order to realize the outcomes you desire. In the final analysis, what makes you a leader is not the title you're *given*, it's the **ACTION** you *take*.

Expect Some Bumps

The situations you face – and the circumstances requiring action on your part – won't come without challenges. Occasionally, you may find that the path forward is unclear (not to mention a little scary). In some instances, the directions you receive may seem somewhat ambiguous. At other times, you may not have all the information you would like. And, of course, there's a good chance that you'll already have plenty to do when new issues present themselves.

While obstacles like these can be disheartening, they're not insurmountable. The best way to deal with them is to pause, take a deep breath, focus, and think. You'll need to analyze the issues, sift through the information that is available to you, and determine the *type* of action that is appropriate.

Types of Action

The actions you will need to take as a supervisor typically fall into some combination of three categories: **Problem Solving**, **Implementation/Execution**, and **Decision Making**.

PROBLEM SOLVING

An unexpected, undesirable circumstance arises and it's your responsibility to get it resolved. This category includes everything from employee performance discrepancies, equipment breakdowns, and schedule overruns – to supplier issues, team member conflicts, and customer complaints.

Questions to answer:

- ◆ What makes me think there's a problem? What has occurred?
- ◆ How serious is the issue? What's the impact?
- ◆ How quickly must it be resolved? What will happen if it continues?
- ◆ Who's involved? Who must I speak to and/or deal with?
- ◆ Have similar problems occurred in the past? How were they handled?
- ◆ What rules, guidelines, and/or restrictions apply to this situation?
- ◆ What are my goals in dealing with this issue?
- ◆ What are the various ways this problem can be solved?
- ◆ Which solution is best? Why do I think so?
- ◆ What (if any) approvals will I need before taking action?
- ◆ What must I do to make sure the solution happens?
- ◆ How will I know if the issue has been resolved?

IMPLEMENTATION / EXECUTION

A goal, project, or desired end-state is identified (by you or your managers) and it's your responsibility to make it happen. Included in this category are things like: implementing new work processes and technologies, modifying/improving the work facility, running special business promotions, launching new products and services, and bringing on additional staff. All of these involve various levels of research, planning, scheduling, and coordination.

Questions to answer:

◆ What specifically needs to be accomplished? By when?

◆ How important is this? Where does it fall on our priority list?

◆ What guidelines, parameters, and/or restrictions apply?

◆ Who must I coordinate with? What (if any) approvals will be required?

◆ What resources (people, equipment, supplies, budget) are available?

◆ What research is needed? From whom should I solicit input?

◆ What are the various activities that must be performed/completed?

◆ Who will be involved? What will be their roles and responsibilities?

◆ What is the desired schedule of activities? Milestone dates?

◆ What potential problems/obstacles should we have contingencies for?

◆ What type of documentation and record keeping will be needed?

◆ What criteria will be used to evaluate progress and overall success?

DECISION MAKING

A task, issue, question, or conflict arises within your work unit requiring a decision to be made ... by you. Whether it's making work assignments, dealing with employee concerns, responding to vacation/leave requests, determining what equipment to purchase, responding to customer complaints – or a myriad of other possibilities – you'll need to analyze each situation, weigh the pros and cons of the various options available to you, and decide what's best for everyone involved.

Questions to answer:

◆ What specifically do I know about the issue? Is more info available?

◆ How quickly does a decision need to be made?

◆ What factors do I need to weigh and consider?

◆ What type of decision is required (yes/no, a course of action, etc.)?

◆ Who's involved? Who will be affected? How will they be affected?

◆ Have similar issues occurred in the past? How were they handled?

◆ What guidelines and/or restrictions apply to this decision?

◆ What are my goals in making this decision?

◆ What (if any) approvals will I need? Should I seek advice from anyone?

◆ What must be done to implement this decision?

◆ How will I know if the decision is correct?

◆ What will I do if the decision turns out to be bad and/or problematic?

A Model for ACTION

The following six-step model will help you take an orderly, methodical approach to situations requiring action on your part. Use some or all of the steps – as appropriate – for the circumstances at hand.

ANALYZE
...**the issue or situation.** Collect and consider all available facts. Do your best to understand what you're dealing with and what is needed on your part. Think before you act.

CONSULT
...**with others.** Collect input from your boss, other supervisors, other departments – and the employees who will be affected by your actions.

TAILOR
...**a strategy.** As appropriate, develop a written plan with specific activities, timelines, roles and responsibilities, required resources, and progress checkpoints.

IMPLEMENT
...**the plan.** Initiate the action you've identified as the best and most appropriate path forward. Coordinate and oversee all activities to ensure you stay on schedule and within budget.

OBSERVE
...**what happens.** Closely monitor activities and outcomes. Request progress reports. Have periodic meetings to discuss activity status and evaluate success.

NAVIGATE
...**your way through necessary adjustments.** Address obstacles and seize opportunities that surface. Make "midcourse corrections" that will help you reach your goal.

Don't Forget to Delegate

One of the most common mistakes made by supervisors – especially those who are new to leadership – is taking on unnecessary tasks ... trying to do everything by themselves. As a result, they can easily find themselves buried under a ton of work. Things move slower, not as much gets done, and job satisfaction is reduced. What's the best way to avoid that trap? DELEGATION! You need to pass along certain duties and responsibilities to your direct reports so that: a) more actions are being performed by more people, more of the time, b) you're a facilitator of, rather than a barrier to, progress, and c) you can focus on – and accomplish – those important tasks that really must be done by you.

As you look at what's on your plate that you might ask others to handle, keep the following in mind:

When To Delegate

- When the task or action is really someone else's to do

- When it provides a fairly low-risk opportunity for someone to learn, grow, and develop

- When someone else is equally (or better) equipped to handle it

- When you are more concerned that something *gets* done and less concerned with *how* it gets done

When NOT To Delegate

- When you haven't helped the person prioritize the new task relative to your other expecta-tions

- When you won't be accessible for any counsel and guidance that the person may need

- When someone is new, too inexperienced, or otherwise incapable of performing the task

- When you truly are the best person tc handle it – due to sensitivity, confidentiality, timing, experience, etc.

A Few Cautions on the Road to Action

Beware of "knee-jerk" responses. When something unexpected or undesirable happens, you may be tempted to react quickly and emotionally. Fight the feeling! Such responses are counterproductive; they typically make matters worse – leaving you with the hindsight feeling *I wish I hadn't done (or said) that!* So, discipline yourself to follow one of the most important guidelines for leaders at all levels: Think before you act!

In a similar vein …

Beware of the First-Thought Syndrome. When solving problems, developing plans, or pondering decisions, avoid the tendency to "run" with the first idea that comes into your head. Instead, identify options for consideration. Your first idea may, in fact, turn out to be your best play. But you'll never really know that unless, and until, you weigh it against alternatives. Just be careful that you don't overanalyze situations to the point of action paralysis.

Beware of costly solutions to cheap problems. Occasionally, well-intended supervisors end up devising (and implementing) complex, time-consuming, and expensive fixes for issues that aren't all that serious. Spending $500 to solve a $250 problem is a bad decision … and bad business! So, mentally compute the "cost" of each problem you face. What's the negative impact (short *and* long-term) with regard to time, money, annoyance, and disruption? Then, examine the cost and appropriateness of the solution you're considering. If the problem isn't worth the effort required to solve it, live with it … and move on!

FOLLOW THE LEADER

10 Ways to Be the Kind of Leader That Others – Including Former Peers – Will Want to Follow

1. **TREAT EVERYONE WITH DIGNITY, RESPECT, AND COURTESY.** Value the inherent worth of each person you have contact with. Presume that people are well-intended. Appreciate the fact that others' dreams, goals, and feelings of self-worth are as important to them as yours are to you. Adopt the mindset that being "a superior" does not mean that you *are* superior ... and behave accordingly!

2. **LEAD BY EXAMPLE.** Model the work performance, attendance, and conduct that you expect from others. Show people, through your daily behaviors, what it means to have integrity, a strong work ethic, and an unyielding commitment to your organization's mission and values. Practice what you preach ... WALK THE TALK!

. **BE FIRM, FAIR, AND CONSISTENT.** Avoid playing favorites. Hold everyone – including yourself – *equally* accountable for following ALL rules and regulations, exhibiting appropriate behavior, meeting ALL job responsibilities, and achieving desired results.

. **"OWN UP" TO YOUR SHORTCOMINGS.** Avoid cover ups. If you make a mistake, admit it ... and then fix it! If you don't know something, admit it ... and then find out about it! And, if you're holding an employee account-able for a wrongdoing that you, yourself, committed in the past – and he or she calls you on it – respond with: "That's true. I did do that. And I was wrong, back then ... just like you're wrong, now."

5. **FOCUS ON *THEIR* SUCCESS.** Provide all people on your team with the information, direction, resources, feedback, and support they need to be successful. Create/seize opportunities for team members to learn, grow, and develop. Be a teacher ... be a coach.

6. **GET THEM INVOLVED.** Whenever practical and appropriate, involve direct reports in decision making, plan development, and problem solving. Solicit their suggestions, ideas, and opinions. Delegate tasks and responsibilities – along with the commensurate authority. Remember: An effective leader knows when to *take* the lead, when to *share* the lead, and when to *follow* the lead.

7. **LISTEN.** Hone your listening skills. Focus on understanding the messages people send to you. Demonstrate, by your listening behaviors, that you *care* what others think, feel, and have to say.

8. **SHOW YOUR APPRECIATION.** Acknowledge and thank employees for their efforts and contributions. Let people know that good work is important – and that good workers are valued and appreciated. Celebrate achievement!

9. **RESPECT THEIR TIME.** Remember that your team members have important (often difficult) jobs to do and priorities to manage. Don't expect them to drop whatever they're doing every time you want something – or whenever you feel the need for a meeting. Be a help, rather than a hindrance, when it comes to employee time management.

10. **DO WHAT NEEDS TO BE DONE.** When you see or hear of something that requires attention, jump in and deal with it. Don't procrastinate or latch on to excuses for not dealing with issues – especially those that are difficult or distasteful. No one wants to follow a leader who shies away from the tough stuff and fails to take care of business.

A LETTER FROM EMPLOYEES

Dear Boss:

Thank you for being our supervisor. While we may not show it all that much, deep inside, most of us really do appreciate the time and effort that leaders put in to keep our business running smoothly ... and to keep us employed.

You have a tough job – probably, at times, much tougher than we think. But it's also an important job. And because our success is obviously linked to yours, it's critical that you do the very best job you can.

Will there be times when we totally disagree with you on issues? Of course! Will there be occasions when we push, or actually cross over, the boundaries you establish? Probably. Will we ever test your patience and maybe make your job harder than it needs to be? Perhaps. But despite how we sometimes may act – regardless of what we sometimes may say – know this: **we want and need a good, strong, and fair leader!**

We've experienced weak bosses in the past. We don't need any more. And we certainly have more than enough "buddies." So, do what you're here to do. Be straight with us. Apply the rules and regulations the same way to everyone. Provide us with direction and support. Be there for us. Listen to us. Give us the benefit of the doubt, but set us straight when we need it. Help us learn and improve. Hold us to high standards. Appreciate us – and the work that we do. Be a role model and teacher ... a coach and an advocate. Be a leader.

We're counting on you, boss. Please don't let us down!

Your Employees

About The Author

Laura Elise Bernstein is president and CEO of VisionPoint, Inc. Recognized as a visionary and innovative business executive, her experience includes leadership positions at The Dow Chemical Company, Delta College, AchieveGlobal, and American Media. Laura's 16-plus years of leadership experience are reflected in her contributions to development of award-winning training programs, her reputation as a gifted speaker and master trainer, and in the profound trust she has earned by direct reports, coworkers, clients, and vendors.

About The Publisher

Since 1977, walkthetalk.com has helped individuals and organizations, worldwide, achieve success through Values-Based Practices. Our goal is both simple and straightforward: **to provide you and your organization with high-impact resources for your personal and professional success!**

We specialize in...
- ▲ "How-To" Handbooks and Support Material
- ▲ Group Training Programs
- ▲ Inspirational Gift Books and Movies
- ▲ Do-It-Yourself Training Resources
- ▲ Motivational Newsletters
- ▲ 360° Feedback Processes
- ▲ The popular *Santa's Leadership Secrets*® and **212 the extra degree** Product Lines
...and much more!

To learn more about The WALK THE TALK Company or to order additional copies of this high-impact handbook, visit www.walkthetalk.com.

Take this message to the next level with these additional high-impact books...

The Manager's Coaching Handbook- This "cut-to-the- chase" handbook provides managers, supervisors, and team leaders with simple, easy-to-follow guidelines to encourage superior performers, confront problem employees, and manage everyone in between. $10.95

Positive Discipline- This handbook contains practical time- tested approaches to resolving difficult "people problems", while strengthening employee commitment in the process. $10.95

Walk Awhile in My Shoes- Revolutionary handbook that helps you break down counterproductive beliefs and behaviors between individuals and organizations. $10.95

The Manager's Communication Handbook- This powerful handbook will allow you to connect with employees and create understanding, support, and acceptance crucial to your individual and organizational success. $10.95

Nuts'n Bolts Leadership- A "how to" handbook jam-packed with practical leadership success strategies. $10.95

180 Ways to Walk the Recognition Talk- Everyone talks about the importance of recognition...this handbook gives you 180 proven techniques. $10.95

For our complete collection, visit www.walkthetalk.com

WALK THE TALK

THE

Trusted Books. Positive Results.

www.ingramcontent.com/pod-product-compliance
Lightning Source LLC
Chambersburg PA
CBHW071757200326
41520CB00013BA/3293